STEEL CITY

XL, XLIII, and the New Super Bowl Era

TRIUMPH
BOOKS

Pittsburgh Post-Gazette

This book is available in quantity at special discounts for your group or organization.
For further information contact:

Triumph Books
542 South Dearborn Street
Suite 750
Chicago, IL 60605
Phone: (312) 939-3330
Fax: (312) 663-3557

Printed in the United States of America
ISBN: 978-1-60078-307-4

All photographs courtesy of the *Pittsburgh Post-Gazette,* except where otherwise indicated

Content packaged by Mojo Media, Inc.
Joe Funk: Editor
Jason Hinman: Creative Director

Pittsburgh Post-Gazette
John Robinson Block, Co-publisher and Editor-in-Chief
David M. Shribman, Executive Editor and Vice-President
Susan L. Smith, Managing Editor
Mary C. Leonard, Deputy Managing Editor
Jerry Micco, Assistant Managing Editor, Sports

BOOK EDITOR
Donna Eyring, Sports Editor

PHOTOGRAPHERS
Peter Diana, Matt Freed, Lake Fong, Robin Rombach, John Heller, Martha Rial,
Bob Donaldson, Andy Starnes, Bob Pavuchak, VWH Campbell Jr, John Beale,
Morris Berman, Albert Hermann Jr., Michael Chikiris, Vince Musi

PHOTO EDITOR
Larry Roberts

ADMINISTRATIVE COORDINATOR
Allison Alexander, Marketing Manager

contents

Introduction

By David M. Shribman, Executive Editor *Pittsburgh Post-Gazette*

Don't get us wrong here in Pittsburgh. We're not blasé about this world-championship business. We've done it six times in football, five times in baseball, twice in hockey. Once, in 1979, we won twin championships, Pirates and Steelers both, and we took to calling ourselves the City of Champions. Even now, the title fits, just as each title seems to fit just fine into our firmament. Overall, we've got a pretty healthy record, the envy of lots of other places. (Hello, Cleveland, how are things going over there?)

But anyone will tell you that the last two championships were special. Pride of the Steelers, you might say. Super Bowl XL was a homecoming in several dimensions—the gifted Pittsburgh running back Jerome Bettis winning his ring in his home city of Detroit, the Steelers crowd bringing the Lombardi Trophy back home to Pittsburgh, where it belonged. Then, III years later in the 2009 Super Bowl, a new coach (Mike Tomlin) with a new hero (Santonio Holmes) produced the old script, a Pittsburgh victory. We live for this. We lived for this before that became a slogan.

In this volume, we look back at the last two Super Bowls. We don't do this because we feel our glory days are behind us. We don't do it because we worry that the heroism of the past can't be replicated in the future. We don't do it because our town is so dull that our days between gridiron seasons are occupied in some nostalgic reverie. We don't do it because, in Pittsburgh, Game Day is some kind of Groundhog Day, always repeating itself.

We do it because the glory of the past explains the glory of our present, and our future. We do it because Pittsburgh is not one of those new cities, laid out in grids, defined by monstrosities produced with the glass and steel we made but lacking in the spirit we possess, filling up and emptying out joylessly with each boom and bust, lacking in history. We do it because, on our streets and in our neighborhoods as well as at our fields and in our stadiums, the ghosts of that past gallop, they whisper stories, they tell us of the ingenuity and skill and pure genius of the athletic endeavor that we have come to think of as our own. We examine the past not to repeat it, but to embrace it, and to surpass it.

In these pages you will see the glory of our days, feel the thrill we shared at victory, discover the lessons we learned in defeat, experience the devotion, the enthusiasm, the sheer intelligence, of our sporting passion.

Flip through this book and you'll remember what Roethlisberger did, what Reed kicked, what Ward caught—and what Harrison pulled in and pulled off in one of the most breathtaking and breathless events in the history of all of sport. You'll understand what one generation of Rooneys dreamed, what another created, and what the third consolidated. You'll see why the Steelers are the Canadiens in shoulder pads, the Celtics of the gridiron, the Yankees of the autumn.

All that and one thing more. You'll understand why this is our game and why wherever we live, whether in exile in Charlotte or in retirement in Sarasota or in residence here in Pittsburgh, we live in Steelers Nation—a nation that knows no limits and has no boundaries, only championships, championships and towels black and gold. Steelers Nation: Sweet land of championships. From every mountainside, let the towels swing. ∎

Steel City Knows How to Celebrate

By Robert Dvorchak

In the halcyon days of the Roman Empire, when a conquering general brought back the spoils of war to the cheering throngs lined along the parade route of the Via Sacra, a slave dressed as the goddess of victory would follow behind and whisper a warning: "You are mortal. You are mortal. You are mortal."

In Pittsburgh, in 2006, when The Bus cradled that silver football in his meaty hands while riding in a canary yellow Corvette with black leather seats along the sharply angled avenues of the modern Sacred Way, a quarter of a million revelers shouted at the top of their victorious lungs: "Steelers! Wooooooooooooooooooooooo."

Hundreds of thousands of them returned to the streets again in 2009, to cheer as Troy Polamalu dove into celebratory crowds with the aplomb of one who dives after interceptions and to scream as coach Mike Tomlin dismounted from his convertible to high-five the throngs.

While it is true that all glory is fleeting and that time grinds winners and losers into the same powdery dust, the Nation has savored its moments in the sun twice this decade by cutting loose with whoops on February days so rare that confetti trumped the snow flurries and the color combination of black and gold defeated gray skies.

The beauty of a championship—as eternal as classic Latin—radiates from the glow of accomplishment, of being the best in the world at what you do for one moment in time, of allowing a fanatic following to raise their fingers in a collective No. 1. And nobody can ever take it away.

Nobody.

Two days after the Steelers won the city's sixth Super Bowl title, Pittsburgh fans flocked to the parade to honor their champions. An estimated 400,000 people turned out for the joyous affair.

XLIII

Sixth Sense!

Steelers win on Holmes' late TD grab • By Ed Bouchette

The Steelers not only have another Super Bowl victory to celebrate, it came in what might have been the greatest of them all, and they have another play and a winning drive for the ages to go with it.

Santonio Holmes caught Ben Roethlisberger's 6-yard touchdown pass, keeping the toes of both his feet inbounds as he stretched out along the sideline for the winner with 35 seconds left. It was Holmes' 40-yard reception with 49 seconds left that put the Steelers in position to win it on a drive that covered 88 yards.

And those were not the most dynamic plays of the game.

The final score in this super Super Bowl was 27–23, and it gave the Steelers their sixth Lombardi Trophy, the most of any NFL team.

"My feet never left the ground," said Holmes, the MVP of Super Bowl XLIII. "All I did was extend my arms and use my toes as extra extension to catch up to the ball. "We're going down in history with one of the greatest games ever played in the Super Bowl."

Holmes' touchdown catch saved the Steelers from what had been a fourth-quarter collapse at the hands of Arizona's Kurt Warner and Larry Fitzgerald. "Sixburgh" nearly became "Sicksburgh" as the underdog Cardinals stormed back.

Kurt Warner threw two touchdown passes to Fitzgerald to wipe out a 13-point Steelers lead in a span of five minutes against the NFL's No. 1-ranked defense.

Fitzgerald scored on a short pass that he turned into a 64-yard sprint up the middle with 2:37 to go, giving Arizona its first lead, 23–20. It came after a safety against the Steelers at 2:58 that cut the Steelers' lead to 20–16.

"I actually was thinking that if they're going to score, that's how you want them to score, extremely quickly as opposed to just milking it," said Steelers coach Mike Tomlin, at 36 the youngest coach to win the Super Bowl.

Up stepped Roethlisberger (21-of-30, 256 yards) to direct a winning drive in the final period for the sixth time this season—and throw his first Super Bowl touchdown pass.

The Steelers took over on their 22 with 2:30 left and were pushed back to the 12 by a holding call.

"I said it's now or never," Roethlisberger said he told his offense. "I told the guys all the film study you put in doesn't matter if you don't do it now."

They did it, especially Roethlisberger and Holmes, who caught nine passes for 131 yards, four receptions on the winning drive.

"I said to him that I wanted to be the guy to make the plays," Holmes said he told his quarterback on the drive. "Great players step up big time and make great plays."

Santonio Holmes makes the game-winning catch in the Super Bowl. Displaying amazing body control, the game's MVP managed to secure the football and get both feet inbounds for one of the finest touchdown grabs in Super Bowl history.

The furious fourth quarter came after what many believe was the greatest play in Super Bowl history.

Call this one the Immaculate Interception, because the 100-yard interception return by James Harrison helped deliver this victory.

Harrison's stunning touchdown on the last play of the first half turned the game around—until it was turned inside out in the final quarter—and it likely created a 14-point swing.

The Cardinals had a first down at the Steelers' 1 with 18 seconds left and were ready to take the lead or tie the score with a field goal on the next play. The Steelers led, 10–7, at the time.

Warner, fearing a blitz, threw a quick pass toward Anquan Boldin on the left. Harrison instead dropped into coverage, stepped in front of the pass, and ran down the right sideline for the longest play in Super Bowl history.

Harrison escaped a few tackles before he was hit just before the goal line. He landed on top of Fitzgerald, and they tumbled into the end zone. Officials reviewed the play, and it stood as a touchdown, perhaps the most astounding one in Super Bowl history.

"It was very tiring but it was all worth it," Harrison said. "I was just thinking that I had to do whatever I could to get to the other end zone and get seven."

Without that, the Steelers likely would not have won.

They moved the ball well at times, but had trouble scoring touchdowns. Twice, they had first downs

(above) Ben Roethlisberger tries to elude Arizona tacklers. Roethlisberger managed to take care of the football all day, especially on occasions where he had to scramble. *(opposite)* Roethlisberger is all smiles after the game, a champion for the second time in his young career.

inside Arizona's 5 and had to settle for Jeff Reed field goals of 18 and 21 yards.

The Steelers managed one offensive touchdown, a 1-yard run by Gary Russell in the second quarter that staked them to a 10–0 lead.

Warner threw three touchdown passes, including a 1-yarder to tight end Ben Patrick in the second quarter and likely would have been the MVP had the Cardinals persevered. He was 31-of-43 for 377 yards with one interceptioin.

With 7:33 left in the game, Fitzgerald caught a fade pass for a 1-yard touchdown over cornerback Ike Taylor, who had held him relatively quiet until then. That brought Arizona within 20–14.

A punt later pinned the Steelers at their 1, and center Justin Hartwig's holding penalty in the end zone, by rule, cost them two points, making it 20–16.

Fitzgerald's lightning 64-yard touchdown came 21 seconds later and turned the raucous, overwhelming Steelers crowd deadly quiet.

The place erupted, though, when Holmes caught Roethlisberger's 40-yard pass to the 6 and the Steelers called their final time out with 49 seconds left.

Two plays later, Holmes made his incredible catch.

"I tried to throw it high, so he was going to catch it or no one was," Roethlisberger said, "and luckily he made a heck of a play."

The Steelers scored first on Reed's 18-yard field goal, but it was a victory of sorts for Arizona because the Steelers had a first down at the 1 and

(above) Santonio Holmes applies a stiff arm to get away from an Arizona defender. The Super Bowl MVP finished with nine catches for 131 yards and a score. (opposite) Heath Miller leaps to grab one of his five catches on the evening.

could do nothing with it.

On third down, Roethlisberger rolled right on a bootleg, trying to pass, and—with no one open—ran it in for a 1-yard touchdown. Referee Terry McAulay, however, overturned the call on Arizona coach Ken Whisenhunt's challenge and ruled Roethlisberger's knee had hit the ground before he got in.

Tomlin then opted to kick the short field goal on fourth down at the 1.

The Steelers did a better job of it the next time they got down there as Russell ran off right guard for a 1-yard touchdown behind fullbacks Carey Davis and Sean McHugh, who came in motion from the left to block.

That gave the Steelers a 10–0 lead, and the Cardinals over the past two seasons were 1–12 when they trailed by 10 or more.

Arizona, as it can, struck back quickly. Given plenty of time to set up as the Steelers rushed only three men, Warner found Boldin wide open and hit him for a 45-yard pickup to the 1. Warner's 1-yard touchdown pass to Patrick brought the Cardinals within 10–7 in the second quarter.

Harrison's touchdown changed the complexion of the game at halftime, giving the Steelers a 17–7 lead instead of perhaps trailing.

In the third quarter, the Steelers moved 79 yards on 16 plays and consumed 8:39, but again they had trouble inside the Cardinals' 5. They had a first down from there and could not get it into the end zone. Reed kicked a 27-yard field goal, but safety Adrian Wilson stumbled into holder Mitch Berger for a penalty to give the Steelers a first down at the 4.

Three futile plays later, Reed came on and kicked a 21-yard field goal for a 20–7 Steelers lead. ■

(above) The Pittsburgh defense never let Edgerrin James and the Arizona ground attack get going. The Cardinals finished with just 33 rushing yards. (opposite) Santonio Holmes is mobbed by teammates Mewelde Moore and Hines Ward after his improbable touchdown catch.

Divine Interception

Move over Franco—Harrison's 100-yard return a game savior • By Ron Cook

Best Super Bowl in history? Check. Best play in Super Bowl history? Check. (I know: which play?) Best catch in Super Bowl history? Man, it has to at least be in the conversation, doesn't it? Best comeback in Super Bowl history? Ah, I can't quite go there. Sorry, Big Ben.

Not that quarterback Ben Roethlisberger is complaining. Not after becoming a two-time Super Bowl champion in the Steelers' 27–23 victory against the Arizona Cardinals that left the 70,774 watching in Raymond James Stadium and countless millions around the world absolutely breathless.

If you ask me, $800 for a ticket to watch this jewel was a bargain.

"Our guys don't blink," Steelers coach Mike Tomlin said after becoming the youngest coach to win a Super Bowl, the Steelers' second in four years and their record sixth overall.

Some might argue there have been better Super Bowls. Legendary quarterback Joe Willie Namath, who handed the Lombardi Trophy to Steelers owner Dan Rooney, played in a pretty remarkable one in Super Bowl III, leading the New York Jets past the ridiculously favored Baltimore Colts. Much more recently, the New York Giants stunned the world by upsetting the unbeaten New England Patriots last year in Super Bowl XLII.

But this one beat 'em all.

Four scores in the final 7 minutes, 33 seconds?

Arizona going from 20–7 down to 23–20 ahead in—what—a blink of the eye? Roethlisberger leading the Steelers 78 yards in the final two minutes and change to win it on wide receiver Santonio Holmes' fabulous 6-yard touchdown catch with 35 seconds left?

You gotta be kidding.

Steelers fans know better than anyone that there have been dozens of extraordinary catches in the Super Bowl. Wide receivers Lynn Swann and John Stallworth are in the Hall of Fame because of theirs on the NFL's grandest stage. But that touchdown catch by Holmes is right there with the very best.

Everyone talked about how Arizona wide receiver Larry Fitzgerald had the best hand-eye coordination and ball skills coming into the game. And he was terrific in the fourth quarter after Cardinals offensive coordinator Todd Haley and quarterback Kurt Warner had virtually ignored him in the first three, throwing to him just twice. Fitzgerald gave his team a 23–20 lead with a 64-yard touchdown catch and could have been the Super Bowl MVP if the Cardinals had held on to win.

But Holmes would have none of that.

He and not Steelers linebacker James Harrison —my choice—is your MVP, mostly because he made the final spectacular play.

The athleticism Holmes showed catching the ball and keeping both feet down in the back, right

Arizona's Larry Fitzgerald gave chase, but no Cardinals player caught James Harrison before he reached the end zone on his amazing Super Bowl interception return. The play decidedly shifted the momentum of the game, the type of back-breaking play that Harrison specializes in.

cept the Warner pass at the Steelers' goal line at the end of the first half and return it 100 yards for a touchdown, the Steelers almost certainly don't win. Instead of either being tied 10-10 at the half or down 14-10, they were thrilled to take a 17–7 lead to the locker room.

It would have been enough that Harrison stepped in front of Cardinals wide receiver Anquan Boldin and made the interception, denying the Cardinals precious points. But the return that followed was stunning. Picking up a great block by cornerback Deshea Townsend, he staggered up the sideline in front of the Arizona bench and made it to the pylon just ahead of Fitzgerald and wide receiver Steve Breaston and just as time was expiring in the half.

"James Harrison was the defensive player of the year," Fitzgerald said. "He proved to everyone in the world why he was given that honor. He's an amazing player."

The return made it the longest play in Super Bowl history.

"It was the greatest single defensive play in Super Bowl history," Steelers defensive coordinator Dick LeBeau gushed.

Actually, it was a lot more than that.

It was the greatest play—period—in all of the Super Bowls. Go ahead. Try picking a better one.

I'm willing to take it even a bit further.

I'm willing to at least consider it for the greatest play in NFL history.

Franco Harris' catch in the playoffs against the Oakland Raiders in 1972—regarded by many as the sport's best play—merely won the Steelers' first playoff game in 40 years. The Harrison interception and return for a touchdown helped win the Steelers' historic sixth Super Bowl championship.

Doesn't that trump even the Immaculate Reception?

Hey, it's a question worth asking. ∎

corner of the end zone was almost surreal.

"Santonio is a guy who just loves to deliver in big games," Tomlin said. "In big moments, we know what we can get from him."

But you know it's a wonderful night when the best play in Super Bowl history almost seems like it was inconsequential. If Harrison doesn't inter-

James Harrison was a ball hawk before, but his monumental 100-yard interception
return for a touchdown in Super Bowl XLIII was a play for the ages

Game Stats

	PIT	ARI
First Downs	20	23
Passing	12	20
Rushing	4	2
Penalty	4	1
Third Down Efficiency	4-10	3-8
Fourth Down Efficiency	0-0	0-0
TOTAL NET YARDS	**292**	**407**
Total Plays	58	57
Average Gain Per Play	5.0	7.1
NET YARDS RUSHING	**58**	**33**
Rushes	26	12
Average Per Rush	2.2	2.8
NET YARDS PASSING	**234**	**374**
Completions-Attempts	21-30	31-43
Yards Per Pass Play	7.3	8.3
Times Sacked	2	2
Yards Lost to Sacks	22	3
Had Intercepted	1	1
PUNTS	**3**	**5**
Average Punt	46.3	36.0
PENALTIES	**7**	**11**
Penalty Yards	56	106
FUMBLES	**0**	**2**
Fumbles Lost	0	1
TIME OF POSSESSION	**33:01**	**26:59**

Tomlin's Tale

Mike Tomlin a man of his words • By Chuck Finder • July 22, 2007

This is the book on the new Steelers head coach. It is an unpretentious, red-covered photo album. He picked the photographs and wrote the red-ink captions, including the description in his second album proclaiming: Greatest Runner on Earth.

"I'd never even read this book," his amused mother, Julia Copeland, said from her kitchen table.

This is a book about football and how it has molded my character, reads the hand-printed opening page.

Michael Pettaway Tomlin
3-15-72

The albums ended with his playing days, but new chapters in his football career continue to be written. He keeps logs of every coaching practice and game through his collegiate and National Football League sojourn. He's always read, from summer afternoons at the Boys and Girls Club to the National Honor Society in high school to his five years at the College of William and Mary to today.

"He is extremely well read," said Pro Bowl safety and Stanford graduate John Lynch, "and not just about football."

In a realm of sideline screamers and an alphabet consisting mostly of Xs and Os, Mike Tomlin is a man of, for, and about words. Speaking them. Reading them. Jotting them down. Carrying them out.

"He's a very creative guy and writes down everything," said his big brother Ed Tomlin. "Probably has a photographic mind, too."

"Mike, he exhibited an aptitude…early on," added close friend and college teammate Terry Hammons, an Upper St. Clair native. But, he added, "He doesn't talk about how intelligent he is."

Talk? For the longest time, he didn't want it whispered, written, or otherwise communicated publicly. His mother got one of those "Proud Parent of an Honor Student" bumper stickers from Denbigh High, and he ripped it off her car.

In his junior and senior years at Denbigh High, quietly tucked among the Geography Olympiad, Boys State, and the Honor Society, he participated in a scholarly competition called Odyssey of the Mind. He and a half-dozen fellow students finished second in the state championship one year, yet he swore his teacher and partners to secrecy.

There are words and images, unspoken and unseen previously around Pittsburgh, that reveal the man and provide a window on his makeup, his character, and his fast track to the high-profile job of Steelers head coach at the age of 34.

Stories about how he came from a single-parent household where they played cards for recreation because they couldn't find the money for much else.

About the birth father he never knew and the stepfather, Leslie Copeland, whose coaching and nurturing developed into his stepson's involvement

The youngest coach to ever win a Super Bowl, Mike Tomlin is also just the second African-American to lead a championship team, joining Tony Dungy. His success should be no surprise to anyone who has followed his rise up the coaching ladder.

Already looking ahead to next year during the victory parade in Pittsburgh, Tomlin is eager to go after an unprecedented seventh Super Bowl title for the Steelers. It's certainly no boast: Tomlin has already proven that he can take a team to the mountaintop.

in All-Pro Dads. About the growth in every direction from a 5-foot-3, 109-pound wisp of a high-school freshman.

About the trash-talking, passionate, intuitive receiver upon whom his college coaches relied.

About the keen football mind nudged into coaching against the wishes of his skeptical mother.

About his second thoughts, after his first college-coaching season, that maybe he should forget football and go to law school.

About the energetic young assistant welcomed into the successful NFL family of mentors and head coaches—Tony Dungy, Lovie Smith, and Herm Edwards.

These tales of Mike Tomlin all reach the same sort of ending: He's a man of his word.

"He already told me he was winning the Super Bowl," said Mrs. Copeland, and what son would

fib to his mother? "'I will be hoisting that trophy, and I won't be patient about doing it, either.' Those were his words."

After years of small doubts, she has learned to believe.

"Because everything you've said so far," she told him after he was hired as the Steelers coach, "you've done it."

He was a small kid. Always fiery. Always loud.

"Audacious," said Ed Tomlin, who is three-and-a-half years older and four grades ahead of Mike. Yet still, as a high-school freshman, little brother Mike weighed a scant 103 pounds. "But he was tough as all get-out." Ed said. "He had a Napoleon complex as a little child. He just grew to be 6-foot-2."

When Mike was 10 months old, his parents separated. When he was 6, his mother married Leslie

(above) Usually stoic but unparalleled in his passion, Tomlin is not afraid to show his emotions when the situation calls for it.
(opposite) Taking over for a legend is never easy, but Tomlin quickly endeared himself to the fans in Pittsburgh.

Working the players through drills at training camp, Tomlin knew before the season started that he had a special bunch on his hands.

Copeland, a former semipro baseball player around Hampton Roads. He began coaching his stepsons in a new game. Then, against Mrs. Copeland's wishes, Uncle Howard Pettaway stole away Ed one day to sign him up for youth football. Mike naturally had to follow once he turned 8.

His mother watched football games only to make sure her baby survived. "I wasn't interested. He wasn't hurt? OK, that's good," she said. Whenever coaches marveled at his speed, she remarked how he was running for his life.

Meantime, the boy continued to take notes:
72 carries, 777 yards, two interceptions, 78 pounds.

1982, City champ, Best Runner on Earth.

Off the field, he built cities from Legos and Lincoln Logs, causing his mother and brother to consider him a future architect. He begged his

mother to give him the same trigonometry exams that she made to tutor his 11th-grade brother, and the seventh-grader finished them before Ed.

It wasn't until Denbigh High, though, that he began to understand the science of how a football when coupled with his intellect became a lever for his future.

"I always saw he could work well with people," said Gail Gunter, his geometry and trigonometry teacher and his counselor on that Odyssey of the Mind academic team, which completed mechanical projects in specified times. "But I never dreamed he would do as well as he's done."

After receiving commissions to West Point and Annapolis, Mike Tomlin decided to take up the Division I-AA offer of the football-rich, three-century-old college up Interstate 64 in Williamsburg: The College of William & Mary. Pro football

(above) Tomlin may have never played in the NFL, but he has been able to relate and identify with his players from Day One.
(opposite) Vocal and energetic, Tomlin's coaching style is reflected in his hard-working and exciting team.

"About Michael's so-called plan for coaching in the NFL," Copeland continued. "When he was at Arkansas State, he told me, 'Mom, I got a plan. By the time I'm 35, I'm going to be an NFL head coach.' And I kind of laughed. Guess what? He was 34. You know he's going to remind me of that the rest of my life."

He was hired as the Steelers head coach after dazzling the Rooneys with his energy, intellect, communication skills, record-keeping. In fact, he had a written plan for his first season. Every coaching day.

The new Steelers head coach described the 15 two-a-days of his first NFL training camp as fodder for the players "to whine about. It is going to be extremely tough. I am not apologizing for that. I'm going to put that challenge out here to them because, in a lot of ways, it represents the journey that we are going to face this year."

In Organized Training Activities, receiver Hines Ward was elected to approach the new boss about the vexing sessions, and Tomlin then took them bowling and instituted the helmet-less practice of Hat Day.

"That's something the Steelers are going to see: He's fun, but the atmosphere is going to be businesslike, too," Dungy said.

"He can be an ass," big brother Ed said with a chortle. "He's going to have his way."

Such as when he pledges privately to raise a sixth Lombardi Trophy for the Steelers?

"After he wins the Super Bowl," Ed said matter-of-factly about his little brother, the new local celebrity, "it'll be crazy. We'll have to do some space travel, leave the earth, to get some privacy."

"You know," their mother concluded, "I've learned my lesson. When he says he's going to do something, I believe it now." ∎

remained the dream. Tomlin put himself on track. He amassed 101 receptions and 2,046 yards and 20 touchdowns and a school-record career average of 20.2 yards per catch.

But before he graduated in May 1995, he realized playing in the pros wasn't in his long-term future. William & Mary assistant Dan Quinn, now the New York Jets' defensive line coach, took a job with Virginia Military Institute in Lexington, Virginia, and recommended that Tomlin follow.

Tomlin made four football moves in four years. "Every time he'd go to the coaches' convention," his mother said, "he'd come back with a different job."

(above) Already one of the premier coaches in the National Football League, Tomlin has guided his troops to an impressive 25 wins and just 11 losses in two seasons, including playoffs. (opposite) The 2008 Motorola NFL Coach of the Year and a Super Bowl champion, Tomlin has many more successful seasons—and perhaps Super Bowl rings—ahead of him.

Harrison's Haul

James Harrison fifth Steeler to be named NFL Defensive MVP • By Ed Bouchette

NFL scouts have a new model for outside linebackers to consider when they scrutinize prospects on the college level.

"Six-foot tall and 255 pounds," James Harrison proclaimed. "That is the new prototype outside linebacker."

Harrison's unique stature grew immeasurably when he won the NFL Defensive Player of the Year in a vote conducted by The Associated Press. Four other Steelers have won the award; three are in the Hall of Fame—Joe Greene (1972, 1974), Mel Blount (1975), and Jack Lambert (1976)—and Rod Woodson (1993) will be inducted in the summer of 2009 after being voted in on his first try. Harrison's reputation shot into the stratosphere with his interception and 100-yard return in Super Bowl XLIII, a play some have labeled as the greatest in Super Bowl history.

Harrison finds himself in good company, although as a two-year starter at age 30, he says he does not belong with the rest. "No, I do not because they did it for a long time at a high level," Harrison said. "I have done pretty well for the last two years. That doesn't compare to what they have done."

Nevertheless, Harrison has become an overnight sensation the past two seasons, the classic rags-to-riches story, a relative nobody who went from no job to two-time Pro Bowl player and voted the best in the league.

At the same time, his story is as unique as his size for his position. The previous Steelers winners of this award were high draft picks: Greene and Woodson each in the first round, Lambert in the second, and Blount in the third. Harrison, who shares Lambert's alma mater of Kent State, was not drafted. The Steelers signed him as a rookie free agent in 2002 and then cut him three times over the next two seasons, although he played briefly as a rookie. Baltimore also signed him and sent him to NFL Europe before cutting him.

Probably the only reason Harrison is here today, besides his persistence, was the broken hand starting left outside linebacker Clark Haggans sustained 10 days before the 2004 training camp opened. The Steelers needed another linebacker and dialed Harrison's number.

"If he doesn't break his hand, I am not here," Harrison said.

Harrison's demeanor was so menacing that even one of his former position coaches, Mike Archer, was quoted as saying he could not wait for him to be cut. Harrison matured and focused his menacing nature on opponents rather than his own coaches and teammates.

When Mike Tomlin came in as coach, the Steelers released another Pro Bowl linebacker, Joey Porter (who led the AFC with 17½ sacks this season in Miami), to make room for Harrison to

From being cut multiple times by the Steelers to winning the 2008 NFL Defensive Player of the Year award, James Harrison's story is an epic tale of perseverance and redemption.

After his spectacular Super Bowl interception, Harrison had to tiptoe down the sideline the entire way to the end zone.

start on the right side. He led the Steelers his first year as a starter with 8½ sacks, then set a team record this season with 16 sacks to go with seven forced fumbles—one causing a key safety in an 11–10 victory against San Diego—and an interception. His 34 quarterback pressures led No. 2 LaMarr Woodley by 14.

NFL scouts often quickly dismiss 6-footers as candidates for outside linebacker, especially in a 3–4 defense, because they are not tall enough. Harrison, though, uses his height combined with his strength and speed to his advantage.

"He automatically has a leverage advantage on guys," said Steelers offensive tackle Max Starks, who, at 6'8", should know. "Then you add strength and speed to that, it's a deadly combination.

"He's either going to fake a guy out or he's going to just outmuscle him because of leverage. You get under a taller guy, you get under his shoulder pads and you just push him back." ■

(opposite) Mike Tomlin greeted Harrison with a hug when he returned to the sideline, but all the linebacker had on his mind was getting to the oxygen tank after the exhausting return. (above) The reason why Harrison—and all the Steelers—work so hard; the chance to hoist the Vince Lombardi Trophy in front of screaming fans is a feeling a player never forgets.

Harrison enjoys a brief moment alone with the Lombardi
Trophy at the Steelers reception in Pittsburgh.

Harrison has the size, speed, and toughness to go over, around, and through players who attempt to block him.

Rising to the Occasion

Santonio Holmes caught a piece of Super Bowl magic • By Chuck Finder

Disney World, Super celebrations, and sports lore had to wait. Early the morning after Super Bowl XLIII, the game's MVP, star of professional football's world stage and stretched-to-his-fullest creator of the play that ESPN immediately heralded as the Super Bowl's greatest, was curling up with his three children and their cartoon friends.

"I just wanted to spend time with my kids," Santonio Holmes said a few hours later. "I went up to the [hotel] room. I fed them. Put on a movie. They were very excited about watching Madagascar 2. We just spent a little time together watching. I really just stayed in and relaxed a lot."

From the tips of his toes to the tips of his fingers, Holmes the receiver earlier had reached out among a maze of three Arizona Cardinals defenders and touched a magical moment. His catch covered 6 yards, a sixth Steelers championship, and an expanse of history.

Strangely, to Holmes, his was an instant of gratification and redemption. On the play before his touchdown catch in the back, right corner of the end zone, Holmes let Ben Roethlisberger's pass slip through his hands in the back, left corner of the end zone.

"It was a play that I should have made," said this third-year veteran from Ohio State. "Ben put the ball where only I could catch it. I took my eyes

off it because I was trying to get my feet down...and just lost sight of the ball. Coming back [the next play], Ben had the faith in me, believing that I could be the one to make that play."

Actually, Roethlisberger looked elsewhere first—a couple of elsewheres, to be precise. Overtime amid this 23–20 deficit was a Jeff Reed field goal away, but why tempt fate after blowing a 20–7 lead? So, seeking a pass into the end zone, he pumped right toward the first option (the fullback in the flat), left (Heath Miller), right again (Hines Ward), and then motioned toward Holmes. He fired. He hoped.

The Cardinals' Dominique Rodgers-Cromartie was in front, Ralph Brown behind, and Aaron Francisco was hurtling toward Holmes. Three defenders. One 5-foot-11 Holmes.

Toes down. Fingertips out. Touchdown.

"I...thought it was going to be picked," Roethlisberger said. "A heck of a catch."

"Great catch," said Cardinals star safety Adrian Wilson.

"Great game," added Cardinals safety Antrel Rolle, who noticed Holmes' career-high nine catches for 131 yards—two short of his career high yet more this night than amazing Larry Fitzgerald of Pitt. "He really showed me a lot. He was their clutch player."

On that final drive, Holmes accounted for 73 of

The Steelers would not have won the Super Bowl without Santonio Holmes. The wide receiver certainly earned his chance to raise the Lombardi Trophy following his magical performance.

Holmes ignited the Pittsburgh attack in the divisional playoff round, returning a first-quarter punt 67 yards for a touchdown against the San Diego Chargers. The score was—at the time—the longest in Steelers postseason history.

the Steelers' 88 yards. On first-and-20 after a hold-ing penalty, Roethlisberger avoided a near sack at the Arizona 1 and hit Holmes up the seam for 14 yards. One play later, on third-and-6, Holmes pulled in a 13-yard gain among heavy Arizona traffic. Two plays after that, when Francisco slipped, Holmes darted upfield on a 40-yard gain to the Cardinals' 6 with just 48 seconds to go. You know the rest: Holmes missed one left, made The One right.

"Santonio Holmes had just an extraordinary night," offered no less a source than NFL commis-sioner Roger Goodell. "It was really something to marvel at."

In the joyous locker room, Miller couldn't recall the name of the ring-winning play: "I can't even tell you, to be honest."

Linebacker James Harrison, whose 100-yard interception return for a touchdown was the longest and perhaps biggest play in Super Bowl history but was eclipsed by the brightness of Holmes' moment,

called the play: "Oh my God, I don't believe it."

Offensive coordinator Bruce Arians said sim-ply it was a 62 Scat Flasher.

So ended the flash of a year by Holmes, the Steelers' playmaker when it counted most. He had the debated 4-yard touchdown to win in Baltimore. He had the 67-yard punt return to jump-start his team against San Diego in the divisional round. He had the 65-yard touchdown play to help beat Baltimore in the AFC championship game.

Then this.

"He's a star of the future," Arians said.

"He can go where no receiver has gone," added Roethlisberger.

"I told him [Sunday] morning, 'Players make names for themselves in games like this,'" contin-ued a tearful Hines Ward.

Holmes earned nicknames earlier in the sea-son when police pulled over his SUV and found marijuana blunts between the front seats. He was

(above) **The spry and athletic Holmes was a special athlete long before he came to the NFL. A top playmaker at Ohio State, his reputation was well known by the time he arrived in the NFL. (opposite) When the Steelers needed it most, Holmes made a huge play. When he looks back, all he usually sees are defenders falling even farther behind.**

Holmes eludes Baltimore's Ed Reed and leaps for the pylon in the AFC Championship Game. The 65-yard touchdown was created thanks to the open-field running of Holmes and the downfield blocking by teammates. The score put the Steelers up 13–0.

deactivated for the next game, against the then-undefeated New York Giants at Heinz Field.

"The next day I came into work after that happened, I decided I would have a meeting with Coach Tomlin," Holmes recalled. "He told me how he felt, and that he said he was going to handle the situation accordingly. At first, I didn't want to hear that from my head coach—I was hoping that he would trust my word that nothing went wrong. But I see he put me in a better situation by handling the situation firsthand"

"You know, when you work the way we work with these players, you're a life coach in a lot of ways," Tomlin said in his morning news conference after the Super Bowl. "You care about them, you do. And I embrace that as much as I do the Xs and Os. I probably get more enjoyment out of watching people

grow than preparing and winning football games. I believe it's what we're all called to do."

So what to call this catch? After all, Pittsburgh sports lore is rife with nicknames.

Holmes pledged, "I'll definitely have a name for that play when it's all said and done."

Anyone for…the Immaculate Extension? ∎

(above) Holmes stretches to try and make a catch in Week 4 against Baltimore. Holmes finished with a team-high 61 yards and a touchdown. (opposite) Holmes lifts the trophy after the Steelers AFC title victory. Following his spectacular performance against Baltimore, Holmes knew that his best was yet to come in the Super Bowl.

Threads of Steel

**Some names changed, some remained the same,
but all provided steel ties that bind**

While the Super Bowl XL victory marked the satisfying pinnacle of a colorful chapter in Steelers history, with the likes of Bill Cowher and Jerome Bettis finally reaching the mountaintop, it also marked the end of an era. Within a year, both of these forces of nature retired after long and distinguished careers representing the black and gold.

Super Bowl XLIII saw the emergence of a new crop of Steelers stars, as James Harrison, Mike Tomlin, and others stepped up—and quickly etched their names in Steelers lore. Harrison's perseverance and Tomlin's stoicism are simply the latest embodiments of qualities that have always marked Steeler greats.

Meanwhile, a special group of players provided steely threads of excellence to tie the two teams together and maintain a thread of continuity. Troy Polamalu, Casey Hampton, James Farrior, Larry Foote, and Ike Taylor remained the nucleus of a top-ranked defense that would smack an opponent in the mouth and force decisive turnovers, while the battery of Ben Roethlisberger and Hines Ward brought that same mentality in abundance to positions not usually known for it—quarterback and wide receiver. Running back Willie Parker, tight end Heath Miller, and kicker Jeff Reed also provided enduring steadiness on both teams, and for their efforts, this select group of players now has two Super Bowl rings.

sey Hampton

James Farrior

ry Foote

Heath Miller

Ike Taylor

Jeff Reed

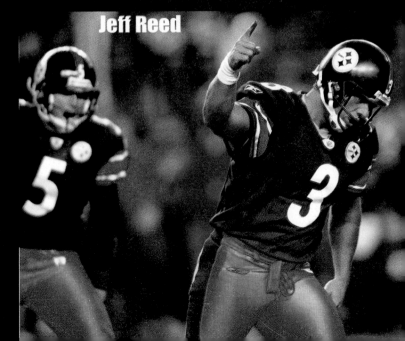

Seventh Heaven

Big Ben produces his own drive • By Gene Collier

Not to be smug about it or anything, but I had no doubt the Steelers could go 92 desperate yards against the Ravens' defense.

None.

I just thought it might take 92 plays. Spread over two seasons.

"The best thing about this offense," Nate Washington said in the locker room of the 2008 AFC North Division champions, "is that we forget."

That happens to be too true. In what was perhaps as great a triumph of selective amnesia as of athletic heroism, the Steelers behind Ben Roethlisberger repressed their collective memory of the game's first 56½ minutes and carved out a monument to themselves.

Washington forgot that he dropped two passes and had his hands on a third that would not have been a terribly remarkable catch. Santonio Holmes forgot that he dropped one right in his belly, that he fumbled another right into the hands of Baltimore's Ed Reed, that he had played most of 60 minutes as though he had no fingers and few clues. And Big Ben forgot those things, too, throwing with typical bravado at his two least reliable wideouts six times in the final 3:36.

It's a matter of NFL orthodoxy, if not actual copyright law, that "The Drive" belongs to John Elway, the Denver legend who is Roethlisberger's idol, the reason he wears No. 7. "The Drive" was Elway's masterpiece, the precise dimensions being 15 plays, 98 yards, in 5:02 to pull the Broncos into a tie with Cleveland January 11, 1987. The touchdown came with 37 seconds left.

But this is about Ben's Drive: 12 plays, 92 yards in 2:53 to beat Baltimore, 13–9. He went 7 for 11 (including a spike) for 88 yards. The touchdown came with 43 seconds remaining.

"Seven delivered," said an emotional Mike Tomlin of his Elway. "He's done it time and time again. A lot's been said of our offensive struggles, but when we need a play, when we have to move it, we have. Against San Diego, last weekend [against Dallas], and now today."

So brilliant were both defenses yesterday, and for most of this season, that it appeared the Steelers and Ravens could play until St. Patrick's Day without scoring a touchdown. In what might have appeared an interminable tug-of-bore to the untrained eye, the teams collected only five field goals over the majority of three hours, and Baltimore led, 9–6, when Mewelde Moore made a fair catch of Baltimore's seventh punt at the Steelers' 8 with 3:36 to go.

It was the fifth time the Steelers would start inside their 10, and if anyone in the huddle of white shirts thought they had 92 yards in them against a defense that had allowed exactly one touchdown in the previous 15 quarters, no one

Roethlisberger raises his arms in celebration following a long touchdown against New England. The Steelers signal-caller has come a long way from his fresh-faced rookie season just five years ago.

The quarterback has been popular with young fans since he came into the league. Roethlisberger always makes time for the kids and also participates in charitable events involving young Steelers fans.

was saying it out loud.

"We were just sayin', you know, 'Keep workin',"" said right tackle Willie Colon, part of an embattled offensive line that kept Roethlisberger essentially untouched in the final minutes. "But look, if you don't believe, it's pointless to go out there."

Ben's Drive started with a crossing pattern to Hines Ward, who made a great fingertip catch for 13 yards with Corey Ivy hanging on him like purple drapes. Ward caught another 13-yarder on the next play. It was first-and-10 at the 34.

Ben threw incomplete to Washington, and then to Holmes, but on third down, with Heath Miller inexplicably on the sideline and Limas Sweed inexplicably not, Roethlisberger threw hard into the left

flat at Washington, who was going to be tackled short of the first-down marker until Reed fell down in front of him. It was first-and-10 at the 50.

"The prevailing mentality," said Tomlin of these moments, "was not so much that we can do it, but more that we have to do it."

Ben found Washington again on the next play for 9 yards, and Moore got the call on second-and-1—the only running play of Ben's Drive—and slithered for 3 yards between the tackles. It was first-and-10 at the Baltimore 38. Ninety seconds remained.

With Ward drawing coverage toward the post, Washington got lonesome on a deep out to Ben's left. Twenty-four yards later, it was first-and-10 at the 14. Seventy-two seconds left. Ben threw

(above) While he may not post the biggest numbers among quarterbacks in the NFL, Roethlisberger and the rest of the Steelers thrive on cold-weather days in front of their home crowd. There is no better home-field advantage in the NFL. (opposite) Mike Tomlin has bonded well with his young quarterback since coming to the Steel City. The two are sure to be a productive pair for quite some time.

Certainly not the most delicate player on his feet,
Roethlisberger still manages to get out of harm's way
more times than not and even found time for a little style
on this play, uncorking a leaping shovel pass.

quickly to Ward on first down, good for 10 more to the 4. On first and goal, Roethlisberger spiked it.

"I looked to the sideline and said I wanted to clock it," Roethlisberger said. "He [Tomlin] nodded. I just wanted everything to calm down right there."

Probably a mistake. They wasted a down, and wound up saving the Ravens some time on the final possession.

The second-and-goal play was a slightly panicky pass to tight end Matt Spaeth, who didn't get his hands up in time to snare it. Third-and-goal found Ward split wide to the right, the primary receiver.

"I was looking for Hines on a quick curl," Roethlisberger said. "Then Mewelde was the second option. I looked up and it looked like there were about seven guys with Hines and by that time I had to scramble to the left. When I got over there I knew Tone [Holmes] was dragging across to the right, and I started back a little because you know I hold onto the ball too long.

"I was about one half of a second from throwing it away."

Instead he whipped it at Holmes just inside the middle of the end zone, and Holmes caught it at the goal line. Not an inch past it. Not an inch short of it. At the goal line.

Touchdown. Division title. Home playoff game.

"It's a special team," Roethlisberger said.

Yeah. With a special quarterback. ■

(opposite) With two Super Bowl rings and a wealth of life experience both on and off the field, Roethlisberger has the ability to become a Hall of Fame quarterback. (above) Roethlisberger was thrown into the fire early in his rookie season, but the tutelage of Bill Cowher helped him to set nearly every rookie passing record in the NFL. The next year, the two were celebrating a Super Bowl championship.

Monstrous Motivation

Slightest slight fuels forever-fiery Hines Ward • By Bob Smizik

There's not much remaining for Hines Ward to accomplish in his NFL career, and even he admits as much. He owns virtually every Steelers receiving record and, with all respect to the great John Stallworth, deserves to be called the best to play the position for the franchise. What's more, not only has he been on two Super Bowl winners, he was MVP of one.

Still, Ward continues to play the only way he knows how—with not so much a chip on his shoulder but an entire lumber yard. Congratulated on his six-catch, two-touchdown performance in the 2008 season opener against Houston, Ward did not offer up an, "Aw, shucks." Instead, with a touch of belligerence in his voice, he asked the media, "Did I shock you guys?"

It was pure Ward, a player who has used slights, real and perceived, to motivate himself to the threshold of greatness. It is Ward's belief that any accomplishment of his is a shock to the world. No one, in his mind, believes he can do much of anything. There's a basis in reality for this belief. After tying for the team lead in receptions in 1999, Ward—a third-round draft choice in '98 —found himself on the second team during the 2000 training camp behind two first-rounders—Troy Edwards and rookie Plaxico Burress.

Ward seethed at the demotion, which was temporary, and used it as a motivational tool. He led the team in receptions that season—catching more passes than Edwards and Burress combined—and has led the Steelers every year since.

He has accumulated numbers, particularly in the Steelers run-oriented offense, that border on the astonishing. He is the all-time leader in career receptions, yards, and touchdowns. With 725 receptions, he has caught 188 more passes than Stallworth and 389 more passes than Lynn Swann, both of whom are in the Hall of Fame. He has the three most prolific seasons in Steelers history with reception totals of 112, 95, and 94. To put those numbers in perspective, Stallworth's three best years were 80, 75, and 70 and Swann's were 61, 50, and 49.

Since eras are different, it's often not fair to compare players of today, to whom more passes are thrown, with players of the '70s and '80s. But Ward's numbers so dwarf any other player's that comparisons are more than fair. On top of all that, he is widely acknowledged as one of the best and most fierce blocking receivers. He prides himself on his leadership role and has handled it well even before being named captain.

He's near the end now, after 11 seasons. But he is not ready to quit—not even thinking about it.

These days he faces another young star ready to replace him as Ben Roethlisberger's favorite target. Santonio Holmes, another No. 1 pick, a superb deep threat and now also the holder of a Super

---

Ward eludes San Diego defenders: The wide receiver has been a steady force for the Steelers throughout his career. During his tenure the team has accumulated 113 wins, just 71 losses, and one tie.

Ward dives for the end zone in the 2004 AFC Championship Game against New England. He scored on the play but the Steelers dropped the game to the visiting Patriots. The loss motivated Ward and the rest of the Steelers, and the team went on to win the Super Bowl the next season.

Bowl MVP award, looks ready to make Ward less relevant. Let it happen, claims Ward, who only will use the challenge to push himself harder.

"When Santonio makes a play, I want to go out and make a play. We both bring out the best in each other. When Plax was here, we both wanted the ball. That's a good thing. When you have two guys who want the ball it can only help the team."

He has nothing left to prove—"I've got every record in Steelers history and that speaks for itself."

In the distance is the Hall of Fame. The fact his numbers are so superior to Stallworth and Swann means nothing. Voting for the Hall of Fame is highly unscientific. "That's for you guys to vote on," Wards said. "It would be a huge honor. Am I a Hall of Fame player? I don't know. I just go out and play." ∎

(above) Sloshing through the mud at Heinz Field, Ward manages to conquer the slippery conditions to hold on to the ball and keep his footing. (opposite) Ward's passion and enthusiasm are contagious—because they are 100 percent real.

Ward stretches to make a catch against the Cleveland Browns in Week 2. He had five catches and scored the game's only touchdown on an 11-yard pass from Ben Roethlisberger.

Despite losing time due to injury in recent years, Ward returned to top form in 2008, cementing his role as one of the most important and hard-working receivers in the NFL.

Ending like so many big plays do, this snap resulted up in a Hines Ward touchdown in front of the Heinz Field faithful. With a smile that is loved by fans and hated by opponents, Ward remains one of the most electrifying players in the game.

The Polamalu Principle

Soft-spoken Polamalu lets his play do the talking • By Ron Cook

On the podium, in front of the prying worldwide Super Bowl media, with at least 10 television microphones about 2 inches from his face, Steelers safety Troy Polamalu was surprisingly smooth, every bit as at ease as when he took that interception back for a touchdown against the Baltimore Ravens a little more than a week before.

Off the podium later, during a brief walk to the Steelers hotel that provided a moment of quiet reflection so rare amid the big game hysteria, Polamalu made a fascinating pronouncement.

"I've never needed or wanted to be a red-carpet A-lister."

Seconds later, Polamalu was engulfed by a throng of Steelers fans outside the hotel. Security tried to chase them away like flies, but a few got autographs, one or two a picture, one older woman even a hug.

So much for that quiet reflection.

So much for that A-lister business.

What a joy—an absolute joy—it is to watch Polamalu handle himself on sports' grandest stage. The quarterbacks in Super Bowl XLIII—the Steelers' Ben Roethlisberger and Arizona's Kurt Warner—are the brightest stars along with otherworldly wide receiver Larry Fitzgerald of the Cardinals. But Polamalu could be the biggest of all, if he chose to be. The extraordinary talent that has him going to his fifth Pro Bowl and, one day, barring injury, the Hall of Fame. The dark, throbbing good looks. That amazing hair.

Think of the endorsements out there! The money!

"I've done four or five commercials for Nike and one for Coke. That's it," Polamalu said, quietly, which is how he says everything.

Four or five seem about two dozen too few for an athlete of Polamalu's stardom, doesn't it? Not that it's surprising, though. The celebrity world still is a place where Polamalu isn't truly comfortable. This is a man who once said: "I don't like prestige. I could go off and live in the mountains and raise my family."

That was back in early 2006, not long after the Steelers beat Seattle in Super Bowl XL in Detroit. Polamalu loved sitting in the backseat then, watching the Jerome Bettis homecoming/farewell tour unfold. He'd prefer to take that same seat this week, but he knows that isn't possible because of his high-profile status in the game. He does better with the fame and is much better at handling the adulation that goes with it even if he fully realizes that so much of it is phony and for the wrong reasons.

If you asked Polamalu, he would tell you, flat out:

"Like and respect me because I'm a man of faith and a good family man, not because I'm pretty good at football."

Since that isn't going to happen…

"I deal with it," Polamalu said. "But I don't really

Perhaps the biggest play in a career that's been filled with big plays: Polamalu celebrates as he enters the end zone following his interception of Joe Flacco in the AFC Championship Game. The 40-yard return sealed the Steelers' trip to Super Bowl XLIII.

Polamalu has been a ball hawk since he entered the NFL.
In regular-season play, Polamalu has 17 career interceptions.

like the attention. I mean, everybody likes it a little. But Monday through Saturday, I'd rather ensconce myself with my family."

And Sunday?

"Sundays are different," Polamalu said, grinning.

The Sunday against the Ravens, for instance. Polamalu sealed the deal in the Steelers' win in the AFC Championship Game by intercepting a Joe Flacco pass and returning it 40 yards for a touchdown. That play—rather, the image of Polamalu lugging the ball into the end zone and pointing skyward—was on the front page of this newspaper the next morning and many others across America.

Even Polamalu will agree that kind of attention is pretty cool because it usually means the Steelers win.

You should have heard him discussing the play, so calmly, so thoughtfully, so strategically. Many people tend to think of him as a free stylist in the Steelers' defense. That couldn't be further from the truth.

"I have responsibilities like everybody else," Polamalu said. "I was man-to-man with the tight end in the backfield. But when you have James Farrior, LaMarr Woodley, and James Harrison all blitzing, you know nobody probably is going to release. When you know your responsibility isn't going to be a threat, it allows you to free up and read the quarterback and make a play."

As Polamalu dropped into coverage, he noticed Flacco looking at wide receiver Derrick Mason.

(opposite) Polamalu runs back an interception against the Cincinnati Bengals. He finished the 2008 regular season with seven interceptions, but did not return one for a touchdown until the playoffs. (above) Although Polamalu has occasionally struggled to remain healthy, when he is on the field there is no more feared defensive player in the game. A true game-changer, Polamalu forces opposing teams to adjust their offensive schemes.

One of the most important pieces of the Steelers defensive scheme, Polamalu relies on his teammates just as much as any player in the NFL—and not just when returning interceptions.

When he saw Flacco release the pass an instant before he wanted because of pressure from Harrison, he closed to the ball, made a leaping interception, then made that fabulous runback.

"We were already winning," Polamalu said when asked what it felt like to win such a big game.

That's the beautiful thing about Polamalu, that humility. Take Polamalu's observations about Cardinals safety Adrian Wilson: "If he were in our system, he'd probably do better than me. He's a better athlete. He's stronger and faster."

Yeah, right.

An eager interrogator asked Polamalu if he thought that his postseason performance elevated him to the pantheon of Steelers all-time defensive greats, the ones with names such as Greene and Lambert and Ham and Blount.

"I'm just another Steeler. Like anyone else," Polamalu said, dismissively.

His words were barely audible, but his pained look practically screamed:

You gotta be kidding me!"

Humility really is a beautiful thing.

Polamalu's humility, anyway. ■

(opposite) No Baltimore player was going to catch Polamalu as he scampered across the turf at Heinz Field. The return truly illustrated Polamalu's play-making abilities as he cut all the way across the field while eluding tacklers. (above) While he usually finds himself in the right places at the biggest times to make interceptions, Polamalu is also one of the hardest hitters in the NFL, and opposing receivers have to think twice when they head his way.

A unique athlete and dynamic presence on the field, Polamalu is one of the greats in the long line of Steelers defenders. A fixture in the city and a fan favorite, Polamalu has found a home in the Steel City.

XL

High Five

Steelers' win in Super Bowl XL finally gives them the one for the thumb • By Ed Bouchette

The Steelers' long search to repeat as Super Bowl champions ended after 26 years when they trumped the Seattle Seahawks, 21–10, at Ford Field.

Playing before a rollicking crowd dominated by Pittsburgh's black and gold, they won their fifth Vince Lombardi Trophy, tying the Dallas Cowboys and San Francisco 49ers for the most in the game's 40 years.

They capped a storybook run by winning their eighth consecutive game, became the first team to win three road playoff games and then the Super Bowl, and finished the Jerome Bettis saga in grand style.

"Our effort today made history," coach Bill Cowher said. "That's what made it special to me: This team has been real resilient all year. It was one guy after another. It's a tremendous group of guys."

Bettis, who rushed for 43 yards, raised the Lombardi Trophy and virtually announced his retirement in his hometown.

"I think the Bus' last stop is here in Detroit," Bettis told the crowd on the field after the game. "Detroit, you were incredible. Pittsburgh, here we come."

The Steelers flew home lugging their shiny, new silver booty to join the four trophies the franchise won in six years in the 1970s.

"We're so proud to bring it back to Pittsburgh," Dan Rooney said.

Wide receiver Hines Ward, who began training camp with a contract holdout, won the game's Most Valuable Player award after catching five passes for 123 yards, including a 43-yard touchdown from fellow wide receiver Antwaan Randle El.

"This is the one for the thumb," Ward said, holding his young son and, as usual, smiling. "We are bringing the Super Bowl back to the city of Pittsburgh."

Quarterback Ben Roethlisberger, who threw two interceptions and had a miserable 22.6 passer rating, nevertheless made plays when his team needed them. He dived into the end zone on third down for a touchdown in the second quarter and picked up another key first down in the fourth. In all, he ran seven times for 25 yards but completed just 9 of 21 passes for 123 yards.

Seattle halfback Shaun Alexander, the league MVP, was held to 95 yards on 20 carries.

The Steelers' halfback, Willie Parker, finished with 93 on 10 carries, most of that on one burst— a 75-yard touchdown run on the second play of the second half that was the longest in Super Bowl history and brought a 14–3 lead.

Parker ran a counter off the right. Pulling guard Alan Faneca, tackle Max Starks, and guard Kendall Simmons threw big blocks, and Parker swooped through the line and was gone. Safety Etric Pruitt,

Super Bowl XL MVP Hines Ward kisses the Lombardi Trophy after the Steelers' win. The fifth championship for the franchise, the title finally gave the Steelers that "One for the Thumb."

playing for injured starter Marquand Manuel, made a diving attempt at Seattle's 40 to no avail.

Parker lit into the end zone, and the place erupted in a Terrible Towel windstorm.

"I just knew it was going to be a great play," Parker said. "They called it at the right time, and Faneca just paved the way."

The Steelers held the Seahawks, then moved in for what looked to be a coup de gras with a first down at the Seattle 11. After two Bettis runs moved them to the 7, wide receiver Cedrick Wilson flashed open behind cornerback Kelly Herndon on the right. But Roethlisberger woefully underthrew the ball right into the arms of Herndon, who returned it a Super Bowl-record 76 yards to the 20.

"That was one where my mind was telling me to throw it over the top and my arm didn't throw it over the top," Roethlisberger said. "I read it right. I just didn't throw it good."

Three plays later, Seattle quarterback Matt Hasselbeck threw a 16-yard touchdown to tight end Jerramy Stevens, and the shocking turnaround left the Steelers holding a tenuous 14–10 lead instead of what might have been a 21–3 stranglehold.

It fell so quiet in Ford Field you could hear the Seahawks fans.

It became deathly so a bit later when Stevens caught an 18-yard pass to the Steelers' 1 that put Seattle on the brink of snatching a fourth-quarter lead. But the play was canceled by a holding penalty

(above) Capping off what was then the longest play in Super Bowl history, Willie Parker leaps into the end zone to punctuate his third-quarter touchdown. The 75-yard scamper accounted for most of Parker's 93 yards and put the Steelers up 14–3. (opposite) Ben Roethlisberger looks for daylight in the open field. Big Ben had one of the biggest carries of the game, calling his own number for a first down with just under four minutes to play. The run allowed the Steelers to reel off more time and all but sealed the win.

and, on the next snap, nose tackle Casey Hampton sacked Hasselbeck at the 34. On third down, Hasselbeck threw deep and poorly. Cornerback Ike Taylor, who dropped an early interception, picked this one off to preserve the Steelers' four-point lead.

It would spark another celebration four plays later.

On third-and-2 at Seattle's 43. Roethlisberger ran 5 yards on a draw from the shotgun. On the next play, he pitched to Parker and threw a block. Parker handed off to wide receiver Antwaan Randle El, who ran to the right, stopped and uncorked a perfect pass that Ward caught over cornerback Marcus

Trufant at the 5 and ran into the end zone for a 43-yard play.

It was the first touchdown pass by a wide receiver in the game's history, and it gave the Steelers a 21–10 lead with 8:56 left in the game.

"They called a great play at the right time," Ward said. "The offensive line did its job blocking, and El threw a hell of a ball."

The Steelers were fortunate to hold a 7–3 half-time lead. The Seahawks moved the ball offensively and smothered the Steelers on defense but had little to show for it, mainly because of untimely penalties.

(above) Jerome Bettis tries to escape a shoestring tackle. The Bus did not have the best game of his career in front of his hometown fans, but he still managed 43 yards on 12 carries. (opposite) Guard Alan Faneca hugs Joey Porter in celebration. One of the unsung heroes of the Steelers 2005 season, it was Faneca who sprung Willie Parker on his 75-yard touchdown run thanks to a crushing block.

With Faneca and Bettis leading the way, Ben Roethlisberger tries for the end zone in the second quarter, pushing towards the goal line from one yard out.

"You can't make mistakes like that and expect to win against a good team like this," Hasselback said.

The Seahawks took a 3–0 lead with 22 seconds left in the first quarter on Josh Brown's 47-yard field goal, and the Steelers were lucky it wasn't worse They finally got something going after Ward ran 18 yards on a first down to their 48. But, on the next play, Roethlisberger faked to Bettis and threw a deep ball that floated and was intercepted by safety Michael Boulware at the 17.

On the Steelers' next possession, Roethlisberger converted a third down by throwing 20 yards to Wilson. Ward dropped what would have been a 22-yard touchdown pass, and a 10-yard penalty and sack pushed the Steelers back to the 40, facing a third-and 28.

Roethlisberger dropped back, scrambled away from a three-man rush and tiptoed up to the line of scrimmage. He stopped and heaved the ball deep toward the opposite side, to the right, the kind of play John Elway made famous. Ward outmuscled Boulware to make the catch at the 3.

Bettis got 2 yards on two carries and, on third down, Roethlisberger rolled left behind Bettis and plunged toward the goal line. The ball barely crossed into the goal line for a touchdown that was held up by a review.

It was the first time a Steelers quarterback scored in a Super Bowl.

The Steelers led, 7–3, and took that to halftime when Brown missed a 54-yard field goal wide with two seconds to go. Brown also would miss a 50-yarder in the second half.

"We're bringing the Super Bowl trophy back to Pittsburgh," linebacker Joey Porter said. "That's all that matters." ∎

(above) Roethlisberger scored to give the Steelers a 7–3 lead, an advantage they did not relinquish. It was one of seven carries on the day for Roethlisberger, who only completed two more passes than he had rushing attempts.

Super Bowl XL Stats

SEATTLE		STEELERS
20	**FIRST DOWNS**	**14**
5	Rushing	6
15	Passing	8
0	Penalty	0
5-17	**THIRD DOWN EFFICIENCY**	**8-15**
1-2	**FOURTH DOWN EFFICIENCY**	**0-0**
396	**TOTAL NET YARDS**	**339**
77	Total Plays	56
5.1	Average Gain	6.1
137	**NET YARDS RUSHING**	**181**
25	Rushes	33
5.5	Avgerage per rush	5.5
259	**NET YARDS PASSING**	**158**
3-14	Sacked-Yards lost	1-8
273	Gross-Yards passing	166
26-49	Completed-Attempts	10-22
1	Had Intercepted	2
5.0	Yards Per Pass Play	6.9
3-2-1	**KICKOFFS-END ZONE-TB**	**4-0-0**
6-50.2	**PUNTS-AVERAGE**	**6-48.7**
0	Punts blocked	0
0-0	FGs-PATs blocked	0-0
174	**TOTAL RETURN YARDAGE**	**99**
4-27	Punt Returns	2-32
4-71	Kickoff Returns	2-43
2-76	TOTAL Interceptions-Return Yards	1-24
7-70	**PENALTIES-YARDS**	**3-20**
0-0	**FUMBLES-LOST**	**0-0**
33:02	**TIME OF POSSESSION**	**26:58**

Forging Victory

Steelers pulled together like champions • By Bob Smizik

The long wait is over. The years of disappointment are forgotten. All those near-misses are forgiven.

There is joy in Steelers Nation, which was out in full force for the 21–10 Super Bowl victory against the Seattle Seahawks. And there's dancing in the streets of Pittsburgh as the Steelers bring home the Lombardi Trophy for the first time in 26 years.

Playing in front of a cheering crowd that gave Ford Field the feel and sound of Heinz Field, the Steelers reached out and recaptured glory. They did it the hard way. They did it the unusual way. But they did it and sent Jerome Bettis, who announced his retirement after the game, out as a champion.

This one wasn't the splendid domination the Steelers had shown in three previous playoff games. This one, truth be known, was a bit ugly. But that makes it all the more beautiful, all the more memorable.

By winning in such a fashion, the Steelers proved just how good they are. It takes a special team to win when it doesn't have its "A" game, and the Steelers, for sure, didn't bring their "A" game on offense last night.

The victory was sweet redemption for coach Bill Cowher, who has long lived with the charge that he couldn't win the big game.

"This is a special group of coaches, a special group of players," Cowher said. "I'm one small part of it. We have a special organization and it starts at the top."

Anyone who knows anything about the Steelers knows Cowher wasn't just throwing phony bouquets at his boss.

The victory belongs to Dan Rooney as much as it does to Cowher and his players. It is Rooney who had the foresight to hire two comparative unknowns, Chuck Noll and Cowher. It is Rooney who stuck with Cowher through some tough seasons when lots of people were calling for him to be fired. And it is Rooney whose unwavering philosophy has made the Steelers one of the NFL's elite franchises and enabled them to now win five Super Bowl championships, a figure that puts them equal with the Dallas Cowboys and San Francisco 49ers.

What makes this victory so unique is that it was achieved with minimal contributions from the player most responsible for getting the team here.

There was no denying the Steelers arrived at the Super Bowl on the strength of the superb play of quarterback Ben Roethlisberger. His outstanding performance in the postseason had turned what had traditionally been a power running team into a passing team. When Indianapolis and Denver came out to stop the run, Roethlisberger made them regret the decision by performing in near-flawless fashion in those victories.

Who would have believed they could win when Roethlisberger played a game that no one thought he had in him?

He completed only 9 of 21 passes for 123 yards.

Steelers legend Franco Harris roots in proper fashion for his favorite team to win its fifth Super Bowl in Detroit.

He threw for one touchdown and two interceptions. His passer rating was 22.6, more than 100 points lower than what he had averaged in three previous playoff games. Roethlisberger's second interception set up the only Seattle touchdown and temporarily threw the momentum of the game back to the Seahawks.

On most teams, such a performance might have ensured a defeat. But his teammates, particularly those on the defensive side of the ball, picked up Roethlisberger, just as he had picked them up so many times before.

It might have been the jitters, not an uncommon occurrence for a young quarterback in his first Super Bowl. It might have been the two-week layoff between games that cost him his rhythm. Or it might just have been one of those bad games that happen to every player.

To Roethlisberger's great good fortune his teammates made certain his performance will be nothing more than a minor footnote to this victory.

Just because Roethlisberger, a quarterback who played his college ball in the Midwest, didn't perform up to expectations, it didn't mean a quarterback who played his college ball in the Midwest wasn't in the middle of this win.

Antwaan Randle El, a quarterback at Indiana but a wide receiver for the Steelers, delivered an almost perfect pass to Hines Ward that went for a 43-yard touchdown early in the fourth quarter and only moments after the Seahawks had moved to within four points of the lead.

The team that was 7–5 and given up for dead by many in early December is champion of the world.

Live it up, Pittsburgh; live it up Steelers Nation. Like the team you adore, you've earned it.

Cowher Power

Indomitable coach finally reaches the Promised Land • By Gerry Dulac

Deep down, when the blood begins to roil and the passion that can make a face wrinkle and a jaw tighten starts to churn, the player in Bill Cowher starts to emerge. Oh, he might look good for a while, standing there, arms folded, playing the part of head coach and remaining calm. But underneath the veneer that is as distinguishable as any visage in the National Football League, he is ready to blow, like Mount St. Helens, just one play from eruption.

It is then that Bill Cowher, 48, a kid from Crafton, can't contain himself. He will discard his headset in the same manner a hockey player drops his gloves, and he is off and running down the sideline, ready to mix it up with anyone he can find. He starts dropping in on sideline huddles, yelling at officials, alternately cheerleading his players as they come to the sideline or reprimanding those who have run afoul of his standards.

"You know what," defensive end Kimo von Oelhoffen said. "He's not a head coach. He's one of us. We consider him one of us."

In a world where idealism is often blurred with reality, Bill Cowher is undeniably a player's coach. He speaks their language, understands their job, knows when to back off, and, most important, has discovered the right way to push their performance button.

A former linebacker and special-teams standout who lasted only five seasons in the NFL, he understands the mental demands placed on players and the physical toll the sport extracts. Above all else, he believes in communication, never denying a player his right to express his opinion, even if it is a contrary one.

"I think he walks that line," said defensive end Aaron Smith. "He's got the respect of the players, but yet the players enjoy having him as a coach. He does a good job of keeping a fair balance between that."

"It's just the way he relates to the players," inside linebacker James Farrior said. "He's been on the other side, sitting where we are sitting. When he talks to us, we believe him."

Make no mistake, though. There is only one man in charge of the Steelers, and his name is William Laird Cowher.

"He's the reason this football team has been able to be so consistent through the years," running back Jerome Bettis said. "His philosophy and his makeup decide the makeup of this football team, so we're a physical bunch of guys, tough-minded, because he's a real reflection of that. He's been that way since the day I got here, and our teams have been reflective of that since the day I got here. I think he's been the driving force."

After 14 seasons with one of the most successful head coaches of the modern era, many of the

The face that was so familiar to a generation of Steelers fans and players: Bill Cowher instinctively knew how to light a fire under his team. Always ready to blow up, Cowher also knew when to back off and how to relate to his players.

Cowher looks on in disbelief during a play. While there's no doubt that the headset was immediately thrown after the play, Cowher's show of emotions was never forced, never faked, and always full of passion.

Steelers have heard Cowher's speeches so many times that cornerback Deshea Townsend said, "I can probably finish the sentences for him."

Now they have heard the one speech they have never heard before: The one following a Super Bowl victory.

Cowher had only one chance before—in 1995, when the Steelers lost to the Dallas Cowboys in Super Bowl XXX, the first time in five appearances the franchise had lost a Super Bowl game. But it's not the loss for which Cowher was remembered. He was remembered for the number of times he didn't get to the Super Bowl.

Now, the coach of the Super Bowl Champion Steelers has cemented his legacy.

"It's a shame, but I think now people are starting to realize how good a coach he's been for how long," Bettis said.

Since the Super Bowl began in 1967, Bud Grant was only coach with more tenure with one team—17 seasons with the Minnesota Vikings—not to win a Super Bowl. That's why Cowher was not satisfied merely making the Super Bowl for the second time in the past 10 years.

"Getting there is one thing, but it's not so much personal as it is for this organization, for these players and some of the guys that have been through some of the tough AFC losses in some of the AFC championship games," Cowher said.

In a season that has seen the Steelers win three

(opposite) The sweetest Gatorade bath in all of sports: the one for the Super Bowl-winning coach. After taking over for a legend who had led the franchise to Lombardi trophies, the win was extra sweet for Cowher. (above) The Super Bowl XL victory cemented Cowher's legacy as one of the premier coaches in NFL history. It was a career-defining victory for a man who had lost in his only other trip to the game and seemed destined to be remembered for the ones that got away.

It didn't matter to Cowher who a player was or how much money he made—he treated them all the same and blew up at all of them from time to time. Although Jerome Bettis was the target of his wrath here, there was no one happier to see Bettis win a Super Bowl than Cowher.

playoff games by an average of 11.3 points and become the first No. 6 seed to reach the Super Bowl, Cowher is beginning to shake some of his playoff jinxes:

* He won his first road playoff game in four attempts when the Steelers beat the Cincinnati Bengals, 31–17, in the wild-card round.

* He won back-to-back playoff games for only the second time in eight attempts when the Steelers beat the top-seeded Indianapolis Colts, 21–18, in a division playoff games.

* And, after going 1–4 in AFC title games, he atoned for previous disappointments at Heinz Field with a convincing championship-game victory in Denver. The Steelers became the first team in NFL playoff history to defeat the Nos. 1, 2 and 3 seeds.

"You don't have the longest tenure in the league for a no reason," said wide receiver Hines Ward. "As players, you want to go out just to shut those people up who say he can't win the big one"

Super Bowl week in Detroit was XL for Bettis, a native of the Motor City who made it to the championship in what is expected to be his final NFL season. But it also was extra large for Cowher, who needed this Super Bowl win to crystallize his career, to bring into focus what he has done rather than what he has not. ■

(opposite) Leading up to his retirement, Cowher had amassed a 149–90–1 regular-season record. During that time frame, no NFL team could match what Cowher's Steelers had done. (above) A relative unknown who had only been a coordinator for three years when the Steelers hired him, Bill Cowher had the unenviable task of taking over for the legendary Chuck Noll. Cowher proved that he's a Hall of Famer in his own right.

Cowher has made the most of his retirement, spending more time with his family and staying in the public eye as an analyst for CBS.

Heart and Soul

Jerome Bettis delivers team to his hometown of Detroit • By Gene Collier

Jerome Bettis barged out of the Heinz Field tunnel for the last time at 12:57 PM yesterday, high-stepping, fists clenched, a joyous ball of quick-twitch muscle fiber aching to command one final standing O.

Unless, of course, he didn't.

Unless, of course, it wasn't.

Unless he has another script in development, another way he'd like to leave this stage, some incredible cadenza that eclipses the three thunderclap touchdowns that broke down the door to the playoffs for a Steelers team that might not have done it without him.

"You take it for granted so many times, being in that tunnel," he said. "I was really concentrating, looking at the cracks, the way the lights look from there, looking at everything, just taking a kind of snapshot of it. Because when it's over, the only way you see the tunnel is from the outside looking in."

The more Bettis tried to explain his emotions and his plans in the hour after he dragged Bill Cowher's walking hangover of a football team past the Detroit Lions, the more it became clear that Bettis might not be sure which way he's facing in the dark psychological tunnel leading to life after football.

He reconfigured every question, lined them up randomly, shrugged them into postponement.

"At what point does your body fail you?" he said.

"At one point are you less a player? At one point do you ask yourself, 'Am I in the way of this franchise going forward?' That's the last thing I want to do."

It was a lot more satisfying, presumably, to get in the way of a team going backward so fast it was backing right out of the playoffs. That's when Bettis grabbed a fourth-and-goal handoff at the Detroit 1 and slammed into the end zone behind fullback Dan Kreider for a 14–14 tie with the dreadful Lions as the first quarter expired.

At the end of a first half that saw Ben Roethlisberger deliver a stunningly flaccid 9.3 passer rating and Hines Ward fail to catch a pass, including the one that went through his hands and hit him in the face in the end zone, Bettis slashed 5 yards to the score that put the Steelers ahead, 21–14. His personal-best-tying third touchdown made it 28–14, and his 3-yard bash on third-and-1 sustained the drive that gave the Steelers another 14-point lead after the Lions had slashed it to seven, which pretty much left players and coaches on both sides in awe.

"I thought about falling down at the 1 so he could get a fourth one," said Roethlisberger, who scrambled 7 yards for Pittsburgh's final score. "I guess I didn't think fast enough."

Roethlisberger pointedly put off any discussion of Bettis' impact on this day, perhaps saving it for a time more suitable.

"I can't talk about Jerome too much," he said.

The final stop for the Bus was his hometown of Detroit—and with it came his first meeting with the Lombardi Trophy. After 13 years of plugging away, Jerome Bettis became an NFL champion in his final game.

One of the best big backs to ever play the game, Bettis' nimble footwork and sheer power made him a daunting player to compete against and tough to tackle.

"I'll get a little too emotional."

Cowher had come into the postgame news conference intent on praising his special teams and looking toward the playoff-lurking Cincinnati Bengals, but when Bettis' name dropped, it put a severe strain on the head coach's emotions as well.

"I have so much appreciation for him; I think he's going to be one of those guys that when the day comes that he's not here, there's going to be a void there because it seems like he's always been there," Cowher said. "I have tremendous appreciation,

more than I can ever express, for what he stands for as a football player but more so for what he stands for as a person. For every yard that he's gained on the field, this guy, in my mind, has exceeded that off the field, the kind of individual he is, the way he gives back. I've never been around too many guys like that."

Leave it to Bettis to bump the head coach hard toward eloquence, even toward tears.

When what was still very likely the last Pittsburgh crowd to see him perform finally got its

(above) A fierce competitor, Bettis eventually racked up some of the best numbers of any back to play the game. He sits fifth on the NFL's all-time rushing list with 13,662 yards. (opposite) Bettis celebrates after the Steelers knocked off the Bengals in the Wild Card round of the 2005 playoffs. Bettis had a team-high 52 yards rushing and a touchdown.

Searching for daylight, Bettis came to the Steelers in one of the most lopsided deals in NFL history. The Rams made Bettis expendable after drafting Lawrence Phillips, who ended up becoming one of the biggest busts in the history of the game.

playoff tickets punched, the swell of appreciation for No. 36 took on monumental dimensions. It chanted "One more year!" It supplied a raucous, moving soundtrack to the Bettis runs lighting up the Jumbotron. It felt, and tried to fill with its collective voice, the void Cowher anticipates.

"These fans have been my biggest supporters my whole career," he said. "The love was definitely there, and I love them back."

It was, amid the raw brutality of this business, an intensely poignant scene, so genuine it avoided the game's lamest cliche. At one point, tackle Barrett Brooks went to the trainer's table and picked up the big tub of Gatorade. He turned toward Bettis.

"I saw him and said, 'No, don't even think about it,'" Bettis said. "I knew the big one might be coming. As a running back, you have eyes in the back of your head, so I was able to foil that plot. That's why coaches always get nailed with it. They never hit a hole."

Of most head coaches, that is true, and so is this. No one ever hit a hole harder than Bettis. And that will be true for a long, long time. ■

(above) Showing off his ample girth, Bettis tipped the scales at 250 pounds. He had one of the oddest stat lines ever recorded during the season opener in 2004: five carries for one yard, but three touchdowns. (opposite) Later in his career, Bettis found himself backing up running backs at the start of several seasons. By midseason, however, it was always Bettis' name at the top of the depth chart.

Bettis reaches out for the end zone while trying
to escape a tackle against the Cleveland Browns.
The Bus reached the end zone 94 times in his career.

Steel City Dynasty

Rooney family makes franchise the envy of the sports world • By Robert Dvorchak

It reads like a script for NFL Films—the epic saga of a football team born in the Great Depression wearing the crest of Pittsburgh on its black-and-gold jerseys, ultimately becoming the city's trademark as it celebrates its 75th anniversary. For Steve Sabol, the keeper of the archives, the plot comes right out of history.

"The Steelers have had 16 different coaches in 75 years but only one game plan—plant your knuckles in the dirt and go after the other guy," he said. "Men who take pride in their power. That's the Steelers. Even when they were losing, they were the epitome of what is so appealing about pro football. Nobody wanted to play them. Teams would win the games but wake up the next morning covered in welts.

"They embrace a tradition that goes back to the NFL's Jurassic Period with the same ownership in the same family," Sabol said. "Their struggle was epic, but the struggle is part of what makes them great. They're revered as an organization. They're everything that's great about pro football, including the eccentricities."

In Green Bay, fans take their football so seriously that they own stock in the Packers. In Pittsburgh, public money has financed stadiums, but there is a unique emotional investment in the Steelers. "In many ways, we always felt the team belonged to the people of Pittsburgh, and we held it in trust for them,"

writes Dan Rooney, 75, in an autobiography that marked the 75th season in 2007.

He followed his father, Art Rooney Sr., into the Hall of Fame in 2000, joining Tim and Wellington Mara, of the New York Giants, as the only father/son owner combos enshrined. And in 2003, he formally turned over the team presidency to Arthur J. Rooney II, his oldest son and the third generation of the family to run the team.

New home, same feel

At the end of the 2000 season, the Steelers did not so much leave Three Rivers Stadium as they packed up its memories and carried them 65 feet away to a new home for the new millennium. With tears and cheers, the transition had all the elements of an Irish wake. In the final game at Three Rivers, the Redskins won the coin toss, and honorary captain Jack Lambert fired up Levon Kirkland and his teammates by yelping, "All right, defense. Let's kill. Let's go."

What followed was a 24–3 win, and tapping into the sentiment on a rainy afternoon, Franco Harris re-enacted the Immaculate Reception as the final ceremony. In 31 seasons, Three Rivers was home to 18 playoff teams and five AFC champions. The only losing record at home came in 1999.

The shell of the new stadium was already up when the old bowl was imploded. When it was

The Steelers' trophies stand tall at a rally following their Super Bowl XIV win. The Steelers were the first team to win four Super Bowls and currently hold the most Super Bowl championships of any NFL team.

The two men that brought championships to Pittsburgh: Terry Bradshaw with his right arm and Art Rooney with his patient and paternal hand. Rooney's loyalty and passion for his team helped make the Steelers one of the model franchises in pro sports.

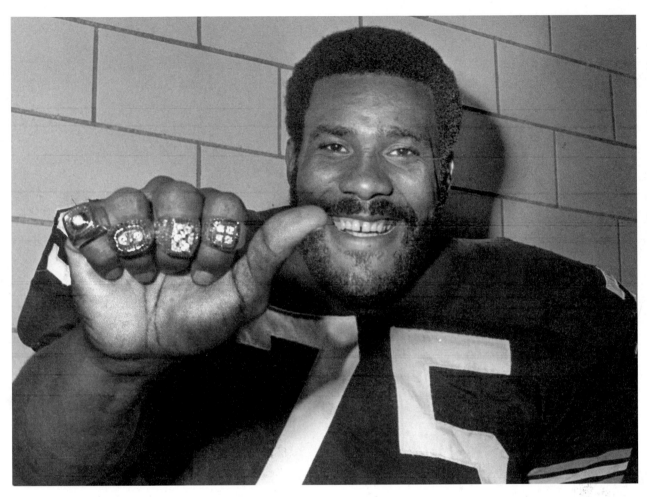

noted the new home wasn't glitzy, Andy Beamon, of the Mascaro Construction Co., said: "We're not going to have dances over here. This is for smack-'em-in-the-mouth Steelers football."

Heinz Field was supposed to open with a game against the rival Cleveland Browns, but the September 11, 2001, terrorist attacks shut down sporting events across the country. It was christened with a win over the Cincinnati Bengals on October 7, the day the bombs first started falling in Afghanistan.

Bradshaw revisited

After a public mea culpa, Terry Bradshaw was named the honorary captain for a Monday night game against the Indianapolis Colts on October 21, 2002, his first appearance in 19 years at a Steelers game. He put behind him the times he was booed, the time the fans cheered after he separated his shoulder, and the time he skipped The Chief's funeral.

At halftime, the Rooneys presented him with a No. 12 jersey monogrammed with the initials of Arthur Joseph Rooney. The ovations lingered through the night.

"I woke up one morning, and I made a point to mend all my fences to come home," said Bradshaw. "I had to grow up. I was, you know, stupid. I was wrong."

Later that year, when he was voted into the Pittsburgh Hall of Fame as part of the Dapper Dan

(opposite) Chuck Noll was the architect behind the Steelers of the 1970s—and to this day no other coach has won as many Super Bowls as he has. (above) "Mean Joe" Greene cracks a smile. Greene had plenty to be happy about when sporting his four Super Bowl rings.

As they always have, and continue to do today, Pittsburgh fans came out in droves to celebrate the team's win in Super Bowl XIV. Though the team was destined to go without another championship until Super Bowl XL, the support of a nationwide fan base has never wavered.

Dinner, he heard words of approval from his presenter and former coach. "Terry is a very special person," said Chuck Noll. "He was a great leader and was able to take us to four Super Bowl championships. He's deserving of this honor."

That same year was the last in the Pittsburgh career of Kordell Stewart. He had once been reduced to tears when he was benched, and he was once doused with beer by a distraught fan. His biggest transgression, it seems, was that he wasn't Terry Bradshaw. But neither was any other Steelers quarterback.

One for the ages

No matter how many playoff appearances the Steelers made, failures in big games spattered Bill Cowher's coaching record. There was a loss in a

home AFC title game and a loss in the Super Bowl under Neil O'Donnell, two AFC title game losses at home under Stewart, and a defeat in the home AFC title game in Ben Roethlisberger's rookie year. The Steelers had set a franchise record with 15 wins, one more than the 1978 team, but that last loss to the New England Patriots resulted in perhaps the coldest walk home ever.

Then came the unprecedented run in 2005.

Four wins to end the season got the Steelers into the playoffs, and three playoff wins on the road got Jerome Bettis to the Super Bowl in his hometown of Detroit. Super Bowl XL didn't win any points for artistic presentation, but the Steelers prevailed by making three big plays—a 75-yard touchdown run by Willie Parker, a 43-yard touchdown pass from Antwaan Randle El following a

(opposite) Art Rooney founded the Steelers and was involved with the team until his death in 1988. His legacy lives on in the NFL. (above) Dan Rooney has seen things get rocky in the board room on occasion, but he cannot argue with the results on the field: two more Super Bowls in the 2000s have returned the Steelers to the top of the heap in the NFL.

reverse, and an interception by Ike Taylor.

As confetti rained down in the indoor stadium, the Steelers finally had a reason to make room in their trophy case. They joined the San Francisco 49ers and Dallas Cowboys as teams with five Lombardi Trophies, and a new generation of fans exulted in a championship that was one for the new ages. Hines Ward earned a spot next to Lynn Swann in the record books by being named Most Valuable Player.

And how did linebacker James Farrior respond when some critic says every close call went against the Seahawks, that the youngest quarterback to win a Super Bowl also had the lowest quarterback rating, or that The Bus may have retired with a ring but he wasn't a factor in the game?

"I show them my ring," he said.

The one constant

At his farewell news conference in January 2007, Cowher addressed the fans: "You can take the people out of Pittsburgh, but you can't take the Pittsburgh out of its people. I'm one of you. Yinz know what I mean."

Later that month, Mike Tomlin became the 16th coach of a franchise that prizes stability and continuity. And in only his second season, he became the youngest coach ever to win a Super Bowl, leading his team to a historic sixth Lombardi Trophy.

Asked moments after the Steelers' dramatic 27–23 victory over the Arizona Cardinals if there was room in the trophy case for a sixth one, Dan Rooney answered: "We'll make room."

A championship is the Pittsburgh version of seventh heaven, and there's no limit on how many will be satisfactory. "It never gets old, that's for sure. We'll take as many as we can get," said team president Art Rooney II.

Jon Kolb, an introspective offensive lineman

with four Super Bowl rings, once tried to define what the Pittsburgh Steelers are. Does the identity come from the players? No—from Mose Kelsch to Bullet Bill Dudley and Ray (The Old Ranger) Mansfield, who died facing the setting sun while hiking the Grand Canyon, they all move on eventually. The coach? Nope, coaches change too. The stadium? It matters not where the Steelers play but that they play. Even the signature industry they're named after is essentially gone.

"I decided that the Pittsburgh Steelers are the people who fill the stadium and cheer this team," Kolb said. "That's the one constant. That doesn't change."

So there it is. All this time, that polyglot assemblage linked together throughout the globe as The Nation thought it was watching the Stillers. It turns out, the fans have been looking inside themselves. They were born at night, but it wasn't last night.

Na zdravie. ∎

(opposite) Steelers fans know, and appreciate, the legacy left by the legendary Art Rooney. (above) Even in the 1970s, Steelers fans knew how to celebrate in style.

Pittsburgh Post-Gazette
ONE OF AMERICA'S GREAT NEWSPAPERS

MONDAY, FEBRUARY 6, 2006 · VOL. 79, NO. 190 · FINAL ·

STEELERS 21 · SEAHAWKS 10

One for the ages

SUPER SUPER SUPER SUPER SUPER

Quarterback Ben Roethlisberger and Coach Bill Cowher savor the final seconds of the game. Lake Fong/Post-Gazette

By Robert Dvorchak
Pittsburgh Post-Gazette

DETROIT

Some will call it one for the thumb, but it was truly one for the ages.

No team had ever won three playoff games on the road and then won a Super Bowl, but the Steelers last night completed a magical ride with a 21-10 victory over the Seahawks, igniting celebrations throughout the Six-Dang Steeler Nation.

And the Bus says his run stops here

Their Super Bowl triumph was the team's first in 26 years and the fifth in franchise history, putting the Steelers in company with Dallas and San Francisco with five Super Bowl wins.

"We were proud of the team of the '70s, but we have our own little niche right now," said Coach Bill

Cowher, who won his first title in 14 years and is the first coach other than Chuck Noll to bring home a championship. "It's a special team."

Although the Super Bowl is supposed to be a neutral site, the week and the game were dominated by towel-twirling Steelers fans who made the game and the on-field trophy presentation a Pittsburgh event.

The championship marked the end of the line for Jerome Bettis, who announced his retirement.

SEE SUPER, PAGE A-4

SUPERBOWLXTRA D-1   HOMETOWN FRENZY B-1   THE HOOPLA C-1

BUSH BUDGET FAVORS DEFENSE, HOMELAND SECURITY, RESEARCH A-8

SUPER XLIII BOWL

Pittsburgh Post-Gazette
ONE OF AMERICA'S GREAT NEWSPAPERS

CENTS   MONDAY, FEBRUARY 2, 2009   VOL. 82, NO. 186 2/2/09 · FINAL ·

LORDS OF THE RINGS

Harrison's immaculate interception, Holmes' dramatic reception seal the Steelers' sixth Super Bowl victory, 27-23

SWEET VICTORY Receiver Santonio Holmes throws his arms wide in joy after an acrobatic catch that gave the Steelers the lead and the win over the Arizona Cardinals in Super Bowl XLIII. Holmes was named the game's Most Valuable Player. Peter Diana/Post-Gazette

By Robert Dvorchak
Pittsburgh Post-Gazette

TAMPA, Fla.

It's one for the other thumb.

Santonio Holmes made an acrobatic touchdown catch with 35 seconds remaining in a heart-stopping comeback, allowing the Steelers to become the first team to win six Super Bowls. It earned Holmes a ring and the trophy as the game's MVP.

"It's going down in history," Holmes said after his catch gave the Steelers a dramatic 27-23 victory over the Arizona Cardinals in Super Bowl XLIII. "All I did was extend my arms and use my toes."

The Steelers, with the league's No. 1

defense, had blown a 13-point fourth-quarter lead as Larry Fitzgerald caught two touchdown passes, giving him a record seven touchdown catches in the postseason.

That lead was built on James Harrison's 100-yard interception return for a touchdown on the last play of the first half, which became the longest play in a Super Bowl history.

If north, east, south, west, up and down are known as the six cardinal directions, add a new twist that sends Holmes to Disney World and brings the Lombardi Trophy back home to form a nexus.

"The Super Bowl is a test, at one point,

of who wants the game more than the other guy," said Harrison, who capped a magic year after being named team MVP and the league's defensive player of the year. "All 11 guys on the field helped out on that play."

Harrison's 100-yard return of a Kurt Warner pass showed how much he wanted it. Out of gas after an exhausting run, the linebacker just made it to the end zone as two Cardinals finally brought him to the ground. The score held up after a replay challenge.

A championship in the Pittsburgh version of seventh heaven, and there's no limit on how many will be satisfactory.

SEE SUPER, PAGE A-4

SUPER BOWLXTRA D-1   A CITY CELEBRATES A-8